Pudding in a Tutu

Recipes and Tales
from a Suffolk Barn Café

By Jacki Smith and Elizabeth Murphy

Contents

Introduction

Our story had its beginning over twenty years ago in a quiet corner of Suffolk, just a short march from the river Ore, when an ancient thatched barn was painstakingly and beautifully restored. In 1987 the hurricane swept through and threatened to rock the already thatched, and nearly finished, barn off its plinth. The body of the building had to to be braced in the teeth of the storm at risk to life and limb. The project was indeed a labour of love with many unforeseen challenges.

For a period the barn in its new incarnation became a tea-room with a medley of itinerant keepers, providing refreshment for visitors who came and went within the small enclave of farmhouse and artists' workshops surrounding it. One day in 1995, our cook, who was not quite sure of her identity as a provider of only teas and cake, took her first look at the inside of the barn and pondered the possibilities. Her life had lately been so much more involved with people than food that it took some thought before she could see what the space might turn out to be.

But our cook is not known for pondering over-long before leaping purposefully into action.

Within two short weeks, having shaped for herself a vision of something beyond a tea place, she had taken the helm of the Barn Café. The mists of the Mediterranean, both east and west, were still swirling about in her head from a former life and were destined to permeate all her cooking. Somehow, too, she had to remember that the people walking through the barn door were customers, not guests. It is possible that this is a lesson never fully learnt.

Over the years, the Barn Café customers begged and pleaded with our cook to record some of her recipes. Visitors will attest that the surprise ingredients of a dish were always willingly shared with any who asked. But write them down?

The answer to this question lies in more questions. How do you bottle a breeze? How do you teach a chicken to swim? How do you herd cats?

In the free-flowing and fast-paced world of providing food, often single-handed, for hungry folk, fixing something in black and white went against the creative spirit of the venture. There was something nebulous, intransigent, and perhaps even a little rebellious, in the style of the 'house' that kept on resisting capture.

In the new year of 2009 the winds of change began to buffet the barn once more. With a possible end to an era looming, as the year rolled round, our cook began to warm to the idea of creating something that recorded the life of the barn and its food. Willing as she was to share all and any of her inspirations-on-the-hoof with food as seeds of ideas for others to pick at, she was at first reluctant to make these into instructions - most normally called recipes.

It was clear she needed a little help.

The task called for an observer and a writer.

I would like to say that I was to be a fly-on-the-wall in order to create this story, but in truth I was a fly held fast in a web. I submitted willingly to this fixative for the space of a summer in order to record as faithfully as I could the intricate strands of this old alchemy: place, people and food.

In keeping with the spirit of the place, this story is the antithesis of a commercial venture, written to attract people in, because the reader may already know that what was in the air at the beginning of 2009 became a reality at its end. The Barn Café has finally closed its doors.

This slim book is a small tribute to the life of an unusual place.

Chapter 1
Beginnings

The low windows, all down one side of the barn, look out over farmland. The horizontal lines of sky and fields are broken by the wobbly verticals of the original gnarled beams holding up the walls and thatched roof. The beams needed to remain, of course; daylight just has to creep around them, which it does very well. The sun, though, rarely reaches into this side of the barn which faces north. The shady cool is so soothing on a warm summer's day. But today, with a fresh March breeze sneaking through its wide spaces and high ceiling, I feel glad I thought of bringing my woolly.

Since I am here, at least in part for the food, and just to show we mean business, we should make a start right away with some warming soup. I don't think our cook will object if we set off at a brisk pace.

Armenian Soup

1½ lb potatoes
1 oz butter
1 dsp oil
1 dsp ground cumin
Handful parsley
12 oz red lentils

1 pint vegetable stock
8 oz dried apricots
1 tbsp lemon juice
1 dsp cumin seeds
lemon zest
paprika

Peel the potatoes and cut them into large chunks and then parboil.

In a saucepan melt the butter and oil together gently. Add the cumin, chopped parsley stalks, salt and pepper and the drained potato chunks. Swirl together and allow to cook gently for a minute or two.

Add the lentils, swirl and repeat the gentle cooking.

Now add the stock and a lid and simmer for about 20 minutes.

Check from time to time and add more liquid as the lentils swell.

When the potatoes are soft, add the apricots and lemon juice.

Continue to simmer until everything is well cooked and soft. Liquidise and return to the pan to reheat gently.

Taste for a balance of flavours between sharp and sweet.

To serve, toast cumin seeds in a dry frying pan and sprinkle each bowl with these and the chopped parsley, lemon zest and paprika.

The dreamy smell of baking fills the air, as two large cakes, one or other fresh from the oven, sit on a wide counter. They would be an advert for passers by to come in if there were any close enough to capture the wafts on the breeze. There are no passers by. The barn is too well snuck into the back corner of this enclave. People mostly come here on purpose because they already know what is to be found or have heard from someone else. I am being unfair to the sign in the road, but true to the sense of a distance travelled as you step through the wide yard and down the track to an uncertain time and destination - unless you know.

The cakes on the counter are carrot and coffee.

Carrot Cake

4 eggs	1 small dsp cinnamon
6 oz soft brown sugar	1 tsp ginger
6 oz white SR flour	1 tsp nutmeg
2 tsp baking powder	8 fl oz sunflower oil
1 oz cornflour	6 oz grated carrot
1 oz semolina	
Oven heated to 170°C	8-9 inch cake tin, greased and lined

Beat the eggs and sugar together using a whisk until slightly thick and frothy.
Continue to beat, alternately adding spoonfuls of flour (mixed with spices, cornflour, semolina and baking powder) and small pours of oil, until all ingredients are combined and the mixture is the consistency of thick batter.
This may not take all of the oil.
Stir in the grated carrot and pour the mixture into the baking tin.
Bake in the middle of the oven for about 40 minutes.
Test the cake with a skewer. If it does not come out cleanly, cook for a little longer.
Cover the cake with foil if browning too much. When cool, split the cake down the middle, and fill.
For a different spicy flavour add 5 spice with the cinnamon instead of ginger and nutmeg.

Filling

1 dsp softened butter or margarine

3 oz cream cheese

5 oz icing sugar

1 tbsp cornflour

1 tbsp lemon zest

Lemon juice

Combine the butter and cream cheese and then gradually add the cornflour and icing sugar until you have an unctuous consistency. Don't beat too hard as this seems to make it turn runny. Stir in the zest, and if thick enough, a little lemon juice too.

Coffee and Walnut Cake

4 eggs

7 oz soft brown sugar

8 oz soft margarine

5 oz white SR flour

2 oz cornflour

Oven heated to 170° C

1 oz fine semolina

1½ tsp baking powder

1 dsp dry coffee granules

Handful chopped walnuts

8-9 inch cake tin greased and lined

Whisk the eggs and sugar together until frothy.

Add alternate spoonfuls of the combined dry ingredients (flours, semolina, baking powder and coffee) with spoonfuls of the softened margarine, beating all together until well mixed. Add an extra splash or two of milk if you have not arrived at a soft dropping consistency.

Fold in the chopped walnuts.

Spoon into the greased and lined tin and bake in the oven for about 35 minutes.

Test the cake with a skewer. If it does not come out cleanly cook for a little longer.

Cover the cake with tinfoil if browning too much.

When cool slice the cake in half and spread with filling.

Filling

2 heaped tbsp soft butter or margarine	1 tbsp cornflour
4 oz icing sugar	1 dsp coffee granules

Whisk the margarine or butter and gradually introduce the icing sugar, beating in between additions.

Add the cornflour and the dry coffee granules.

Beat well together and adjust for flavour and thickness.

Depending on the kind of coffee granules used, the filling may still be very pale with flecks of coffee running through it. These flecks have a slight crunchy bite and give bursts of flavour as you eat. If this is not to your taste dissolve the coffee granules in the smallest quantity of hot water before adding to the filling

There is a group of four people, who sit comfortably round coffee cups and empty plates, at one of the smaller scrubbed-wood tables. There are not many tables in this the body of the barn, enough for twenty or so to sit in different-sized groups. To maximise the seating they are arranged in a chummy way with chair legs mingling.

The counter-with-cakes divides off the business end of the room and gives way to a door into the kitchen.

The visitors gather me in with smiles as I am introduced by our cook as a friend. So friends of 'the Barn' meet another kind of friend. I would like to say *I am really the fly on the wall,* just to warn them that I might not be quite what I seem, but I don't.

A picture has been commissioned by one half of the group from the artist whose work has, for many years, found a gallery on the walls of the barn. She is here with her husband. The completed picture has been handed over today.

The commissioning couple wanted, and have now received, a very personal memento of the Barn, with its steep thatched roof and stable door; an image to remind them of their many visits. A simple photograph was clearly never going to be sufficient.

Our cook, caught up in the moment, is shedding a quiet tear at the unexpected kindness of the couple who have asked the artist to also make a smaller version of the painting just for her. She doesn't say, but I know there is a meaningful prescience in the gift. She may not be the custodian of the barn for much longer. This, of course, is why I am here.

I think we need a reason to smile.

Potato Croquettes *(I'm not calling them balls)*

With a quantity of mashed potato for 6 hungry people add a handful of cardamom seeds, a fist of chopped mint, 2 small or banty eggs and a pour of cream. Beat and adjust cream and egg to make a smooth but not too soggy mash.
Make balls of mash in the hands and roll to cover in olive oil and then breadcrumbs.
Fry briskly and briefly, in hot butter and oil mixed, to make a crispy outer.
Cook in small batches and put in the oven to keep warm until ready to use.

The 'arty' moment is my undoing.

Within so few minutes of stepping over the threshold, armed with carefully planned determination to be a cool observer for the duration of this project, I am being tumbled in a tide. Spun head over heels, I land on an unexpected shore. The barn begins to take on strange magical properties in my mind. These properties start to defy the solidity and physicality of its weather-board walls and extend symbolic fingers deep and far into human realms. The barn ceases to be just a building and starts to be something so intricately woven with people that it has purpose and personality in its own right. It becomes in my mind *the Barn*.

As a writer I am required to reconstruct a world where nothing is coincidental; everything must be connected and make sense. So which arch-arranger could it be who wanted to bring something meaty to my watch today and change the way I saw this place?

Can I suspect our cook? I take it as a sign to suspend my natural scepticism and go with the flow. However, since we are on the theme of the unexpected here is a pie with unexpected ingredients.

Cauliflower, Celery, Walnut and *Pear* Pie

4 conference pears	*2 tsp sesame seeds*
2 sticks celery	*single cream*
1 medium cauliflower	*salt and pepper*
3 oz dates	*fresh oregano*
2 tbsp walnuts	*large orange*
Half quantity of short crust pastry (see next recipe)	
Oven heated to 180ºC	*Medium sized rectangular tin or oven dish*

Peel the pears and quarter them and place in a baking dish.

Simmer the chopped celery, with a tablespoon of water and a small corner of butter, in a pan with a lid until slightly softened.

Cook the cauliflower florets, drain well and then pile both of the vegetables onto the pears.

Scatter the chopped dates over the top. Pour over the single cream to make a thin layer on the bottom of the dish.

Sprinkle with salt and pepper, chopped oregano and zest of orange.

Toast chunky chopped walnuts and sesame seeds in a dry frying pan and make this the final layer in the dish before covering with a layer of shortcrust pastry.

Bake for about 20 minutes until the pastry is golden

I perch on a stool in the kitchen. There are no corners in this compact room. Every inch of space is needed for preparing food for up to twenty people at a time so I sit in a spot where I am least in the way. This is in the doorway into the main barn and beside a fridge. It is not the principal fridge though. And there is a chilling draught.

The essence of barn overspills into this kitchen. It feels as if someone has cooked in it for hundreds of years. It neither gleams nor sparkles. There are no frivolous machines. It is furnished with the practical and simple. Its equipment has seen steady service over the fourteen years of our cook's time here and was probably rescued or gifted second hand before that. It's only replaced when completely broken or unusable.

The history of the cooker is known to me personally, a free-standing perfectly functional device unwanted by a member of my own family. But it is quite old. It has been given a resting place in this kitchen because it works and it was desperately needed. There are no Aga romances here.

There is one main working surface with a window above, looking south, out over the courtyard and towards the possible arrival of customers. The sun beams in through the panes and gives the kitchen a comfortable glow. The window makes this galley of a kitchen into a crows nest too, when we already knew it was the cockpit of the establishment, with our captain steering her solo course through calm and storm.

There is a tiny additional surface, one just wide enough to roll out some pastry, beside my stool. I will be in the way if it is needed.

Which it is.

Shortcrust Pastry

1lb of flour (mix different types: wholemeal, rye, spelt but always include some white to help make the pastry more manageable).
8 oz fat (butter and white fat mixed).
2 egg yolks

Cut the fat through the flour and turn into crumbs with the knife or your fingers.
Bind with the egg yolks and a little cold water to make a dough.
Leave the pastry to rest in the fridge for 20 minutes and then roll as needed.
If the pastry doesn't roll easily help by patting or 'heeling' it gently round the tin/dish.
This quantity is enough to make two savoury tarts so either make it as it stands and freeze half of the pastry ready for another day, or make half the quantity.
Also, when baking blind, lay 2 forks across the width of the base whilst the pastry is cooked in the oven - a quick way of helping it keep its shape in the tin.

At its simplest, I am here to record the recipes that are never written down by our cook but grow organically out of a well of experience and intuition. The journey has been a learning process, she assures me, born of necessity and the need to earn a living. She 'happened' upon a formula that worked and drew people back to her barn again and again.

Cook, this smacks of too much modesty.

I will flex my writer's muscles and say quite definitively: *There is more to this than accident.*

I am not here just for the recipes though, important as they are. I am also here to attempt to draw a picture of an extraordinary chunk of life as it crisses and crosses its way through the walls of this barn, which we now know has become the Barn.

As we get down to more recipes in the kitchen, the air crackles a little, and not because something is under the grill.

The cook is nibbled by qualms because she knows her style of cooking does not lend itself to recording and precision. That is why there has never been any attempt at setting anything down on paper before.

I am nervous because how can I possibly distil the spirit of this place and time, and put it into words?

We both feel we are launching ourselves into something unknown and dimly seen.

The cooking begins with a rush and lightning hands. There seem to be several dishes happening at once.

I should be more organised and have things prepared for you.

I sit with pen and paper and wait for the hum to die down.

Just do what you normally do. This will be just what it is. It mustn't be contrived.

I am surprised at my outer calmness.

So here is something upside down.

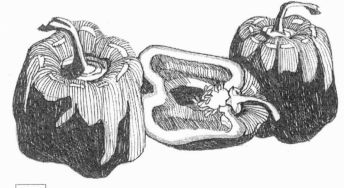

Roast Vegetable Tatin

Serves 4-6

5-6 large mixed root vegetables (sweet potato, celeriac, parsnip etc)

1 butternut squash	1 oz butter
Heart of 1 large leek	2 mugs soft apricots
Fennel and coriander seeds	Fresh coriander
4-5 garlic cloves	Zest of lemon
2½ tbsp brown sugar	
½ quantity shortcrust pastry (see above)	Medium sized rectangular tin or oven dish
Oven heated to 180° C	

Dice the mix of root vegetables and butternut squash into 1-2 inch cubes. Parboil in salted water and add the sliced heart of leek (save the green for soup) for the last few minutes.

Scatter a handful each of fennel and coriander seeds into a large rectangular roasting tin with some whole garlic cloves. Drain the vegetables, tip into the tin and sprinkle with the olive oil. Roast in the oven mixing and turning a couple of times until cooked and tinged with brown.

In a pan boil 2 mugs of water with the brown sugar and butter until reduced by about a half. Add the apricots, sliced through, and simmer together for about 10 minutes. Taste and add black pepper and salt as wished.

Spread the apricots over the roast vegetables. Then reduce the syrup a little more if not already a thick consistency and finally pour this over the vegetables and apricots.

Sprinkle a layer of rough chopped coriander, stalks and all, over the vegetables and cover with a layer of thinly rolled pastry.

Bake for 20 minutes and serve with grated lemon rind on the crust.

The idea is, of course, being a tarte tatin, that it should be turned upside down to serve but this is really a question of preference and it can be served either way up! Our cook rather likes to serve it with the golden and crusty side up.

We begin to talk about ingredients. The majority of our cook's food comes from as many local suppliers as she can find - and always has done. In the summer months a quantity of her vegetables and herbs are from her own garden or friends' and, by default, are often then also organic, as well as little travelled. Her intention is not so much fuelled by the recent appraisal of our crazy food miles but because local shopping brings useful networks, good turns returned, an economy of purpose and result. Always the cementing of human links.

It all makes so much more sense.

I can see how everything fits together with the barn and the cooking at the centre.

As our cook chops away the green parts of the leek to save for soup and the heart goes in amongst the vegetables for the tart, she explains how she tries to waste as little as possible.

Even a single haricot bean, it's so small in one way but it also has the potential to be something more than itself, and has to be treated with care.

Whispered in hushed religious tones? Ah no, the words are said with a vigorous nod to reality. The grit of that reality is our responsibility to the world and the overarching need to make ends meet.

If there is a religion here it amounts to this: food can be good, plentiful and delicious but this bears no relationship to how much it has cost.

So how about a touch of modest luxury.

Pot Roast Beef

Serves 6

3½ lb rolled brisket	*2 fat garlic cloves*
1 large wine glass red wine	*6 oz odd cuts bacon*
3 tbsp olive oil	*Meat stock*
1 tbsp mixed herbs	*1 dsp tomato purée*
2 sticks celery	*Grated zest of orange*
2 large onions	
1 large carrot	*Oven heated to 180°C*

Marinate the beef in the wine, oil, and herbs overnight.

The next day, chop the celery, onion, carrot, garlic and bacon bits.

Cook these briskly in a lightly oiled pan with the lid on for about 10 minutes.

Prepare a large sheet of tinfoil big enough to wrap the meat in and lay it across a roasting tin that is just slightly larger than the piece of beef.

Remove the meat from the marinade and place in the middle of the foil. Pour the vegetables and half the marinade over and around the beef. Wrap up firmly in the foil and add a cupful of water around the parcel to stop it sticking to the tin.

Place in the oven for 20 minutes at the full temperature and then reduce to 130°C for 2 hours.

Turn the parcel of meat over. It doesn't matter if some juices escape into the tin at this point. Add more water to the tin if the liquid has dried up. Cook for 30 minutes more.

Remove from the oven and leave the beef to 'rest' on a platter while you pour the marinade and meat juices into a pan, adding some meat stock, the tomato purée and seasoning.

Allow it to simmer gently until thickened to preferred consistency.

Serve the beef sliced, with the sauce poured over and scattered with grated orange zest.

This dish could be served with the *Potato Croquettes* which appeared a little earlier in this chapter and:

Roasted Beetroot and Squash

Serves 6

4 medium beetroot	*4 tbsp olive oil*
2 medium butternut squash	*Seasoned flour*
6-8 unpeeled whole garlic cloves	*Fresh tarragon*
Oven heated to 180°	

Boil the beetroot for about 45 minutes until a sharp knife can be inserted with just a little resistance.

Drain and peel and dice the beetroot as soon as they can be handled.

Peel and dice the butternut squash.

Place both vegetables together in a roasting tin.

Scatter the garlic cloves, whole and unpeeled, in the tin too.

Sprinkle with the oil and the seasoned flour.

Roast for about 40 minutes, turning the vegetables halfway thorough the cooking time.

When the cooking is complete the garlic skin can be removed by pressing down on each clove with a fork which allows the creamy garlic inside to escape and be mixed into the other vegetables.

Scatter with the chopped tarragon to serve.

Spring Greens (for more colour)

A quantity of lightly steamed spring greens. Stir fry briefly with grated ginger, chopped chilli and garlic and serve.

More dishes begin to take shape. There is time to talk and to record. There is even time to serve a couple who have come for coffee and scones. The woman can't eat seeds so our cook delves for some seedless homemade jam and the personal care is returned when they alert our cook to the possibility that her huge brown hound of a dog might be about to choke on the end of a bone. Thankfully there is no emergency.

We return to the cooking and the talk. I learn that she considers many of the combinations of ingredients in her dishes to be fortuitous accidents arising out of the need to find a replacement for something missing in her cupboard. That is exactly how cornflour and semolina come to be blended with regular flour in her baking. A personal deviation which she hopes adds a distinctive bite and depth to her cakes.

Don't call them sponges she says.

And then there's the sorrel.

So you take a few handfuls of spinach mixed with sorrel, our cook calmly explains as she starts out on the next recipe.

Sorrel?

Dare I admit that I have only a vague idea of what sorrel is? Why should it go with spinach as if it is fish with chips? Then I understand. Sorrel just happens to grow amongst her spinach and when she picks one she gathers the other and loves the sharp rhubarb and lemon flavours it adds to her dishes.

Perhaps it grows in your spinach patch too.

I also discover that our cook considers certain uncooked vegetables, in particular peppers and cucumber, which I relish in their raw state, as totally indigestible. Clearly not a *complete* meeting of minds on this project. I will try not to let it affect the tone of the recipes.

Spinach Stuffed Sweet Peppers (Cooked)

Serves 4

4 sweet peppers (any colour)	*¼ pint vegetable stock*
1 lb spinach (with or without sorrel)	*1 dsp grated fresh ginger*
1 tbsp olive oil	*Handful fresh coriander*
4 oz cous cous	*Handful toasted pinenuts*
2 oz raisins	*Handful toasted sesame seeds*
1 tsp cumin	*Zest of a lemon and a lime*
Corner of butter	
Oven heated to 180°C	

Bring a pan of water to the boil and cook the peppers whole for 5 minutes. Plunge them immediately into cold water in order to set the colour.

Drain, remove the stalk and the seeds from the top (without splitting in half) and place the peppers in an oven proof dish. Sprinkle with the olive oil and roast for 10 minutes. Meanwhile, lightly steam the spinach and then drain thoroughly. Chop through a little. Place the cous cous in a bowl with the raisins, cumin, butter and pour over the boiling vegetable stock. Cover the bowl and leave to swell. This will take about 10 minutes.

Fluff up the cous cous with a fork and add the spinach, ginger and chopped coriander. Season to taste.

Fill the peppers with the mix and arrange in the oven proof dish. Sprinkle the sesame seeds and pinenuts over the top and warm through in the oven to serve. These are also good eaten cold with a strong mustard and lemon dressing.

Chapter 2
Best fork forward

The sun is shining full on. Lush and electric, the spring greens are still new enough to surprise my eyes as I get out of the car. The huge brown hound, a unique recipe of Spinone and chocolate Labrador, lopes round the corner of the barn to greet me. He strains at his tether, sniffs at me and then lollops back to his resting place. There is a complete stillness in the building today. Too much stillness I think. There are no signs of any customers.

Nobody. Not a soul. Not since Sunday

I learn there were two groups on Sunday. One of them materialised after a late morning phone call to book in thirteen for lunch. I sense the tension between providing for the unexpected at a moment's notice, and producing food that waits for those who never come. Then ingenuity of every kind must step in. Dishes can be frozen for later use. Impromptu suppers at home with friends bubble up in the wake of quiet days at the Barn.

As I hover around the merest possibility of wasted food I quickly see that this is a very sensitive topic. The expression on our cook's face suggests thorns under her nails.

Strangely, what might be the happiest resolution to this problem is an unexpected contradiction to the spontaneous spirits which float here: a degree of planning from those who would like to eat. A warning phone call to book a time and a number. And a chance for the cook to provide amply without fear of the greedy maw of the bin looming in the back of her mind, even though it is the very last place food would ever end up.

She does keep chickens. But I wonder to myself whether a pig might not be more help.

Sunday lunch has been an affair of lingering food, chatter and laughter round the largest scrubbed table at one end of the barn. I have not seen this occasion in particular but I have seen several like it. I know it is the sum of many parts. I know that the food and the place are a means to an end; a way of creating time and space for people to share a moment together that will not be easily forgotten.

A long luscious Sunday lunch for you too.

Chicken Liver Paté

1 lb chicken livers	1 tsp ground nutmeg
Milk	2 sprigs fresh or 1 small tsp dried thyme
9 rashers smoked streaky bacon	½ tsp ground black pepper
Bay leaves	Salt
1½ oz butter	2 tbsp brandy
1 small onion	2 egg yolks
1 fat clove garlic (2 if skinny)	2 tbsp cream
Food processor	Oven heated to 150° C

Cover the chicken livers with milk in a bowl, mix around and leave for 15 minutes or so.

Take a largish loaf tin or dish (approx 2 lb size) and line the bottom with a few bay leaves and then 2-3 rashers of the bacon.

Chop onion and garlic and cook gently in butter with a small pour of olive oil added. When sizzling and starting to soften, snip in the remaining bacon rashers and add spices, seasoning and chopped herb.

Drain the milk off the livers (save the milk for a cat) and toss the meat into the onion and bacon mix.

Let the liquid bubble away and evaporate, turning the livers so that they lightly brown on all sides.

Add the brandy and allow them to cook together for a minute or two.

Spoon or tip this mixture into the processor and then leave for a few minutes to cool slightly.

Add the egg yolks and the cream. Whizz until blended but not completely smooth.

Pour the mixture into the loaf tin, place a greased paper on the top and sit the tin in a tray of water (Bain Marie).

Bake in the oven for about 30 minutes until set. Turn the oven off and leave the paté inside until the oven is cold.

Turn out of the tin and wrap ready to chill and store in the fridge.

Elizabethan Pork

Serves 6

3lb pork - shoulder or leg	*12 sage leaves or 1 dsp dried sage*
2 onions	*2 sprigs of fresh or 1 dsp dried rosemary*
3 sticks celery	*2 sprigs fresh or 1 dsp dried oregano*
1 scant dsp curry powder	*1lb mix of dates, apricots and tart apple*
1 dsp fennel seeds	*Zest from 1 orange and 1 lemon*
1 heaped tsp ginger	*½ bottle red wine*
1 heaped tsp nutmeg	*Oven heated to 130°C*

Prepare and cut the meat into rough 2 inch cubes if not already done by your butcher.

Chop onions and celery and start cooking gently in a large pan (that has a lid) with a pour of oil. Add all of the herbs (chopped) and spices one by one, stirring and amalgamating with the onion, and releasing the flavours over the heat. Season with about a teaspoon each of salt and pepper.

Remove the onion mix with a draining spoon, into a bowl on one side, and turn up the heat under the remaining oil. Now brown the cubes of pork briskly on all sides, a small quantity at a time.

Return all of the pork and the onion mix to the pan.

Chop the dates, apricots and apple, and add to the pan followed by the orange and lemon zest.

Pour over the red wine and top up with some stock if the upper cubes of pork are not immersed in liquid.

Bring gently to the boil.

Cover with the lid and simmer slowly on top of the stove for about an hour. Test to see if pork pulls apart easily, if not cook some more.

If preferred, cook in a covered casserole in the oven at 130°C for an hour.

If, at the end of the cooking time, the liquid round the meat is too thin, remove the pork and boil to reduce and thicken it to a sauce consistency. Alternatively thicken the juices with a little cornflour.

Serve with scattered orange zest and chopped flat leaf parsley.

This dish benefits from cooking a day in advance.

French Potatoes

Serves 6-8

1 clove garlic
2 oz butter
2 lb waxy potatoes
1 pint single cream
Oven heated to 180°C

¼ pint milk
1 tsp grated nutmeg
2 bay leaves

Medium size rectangular tin or oven dish

Wipe a split garlic round the sides of a roasting tin or dish and smear with half of the butter.

Peel and slice the potatoes thinly.

Layer the potatoes into the tin with nuggets of butter in between the layers.

Bring the cream, mixed with the milk, to the boil and infuse with the grated nutmeg, 2 bay leaves and salt and pepper.

Pour this over the potatoes, cover with foil and bake for about 40 minutes.

Uncover the potatoes and test to see if they are soft. Re-cover and return to the oven for longer if they are not.

When all the potatoes are soft, remove the foil, moisten the top layer and return to the oven at 130°C for 10 minutes until lightly golden.

Broccoli with Attitude

Serves 6

1 lb broccoli
2 leeks
1 clove garlic
Fennel seeds

Tin of chopped tomatoes
1 tsp red wine vinegar
Lemon zest
Fresh parsley

Slice the broccoli stalks into rounds and parboil with the divided heads for about 5 minutes.

Prepare and chop through the leeks into small slices and cook gently with the chopped garlic and a fistful of fennel seeds in some butter in a pan.

When the leeks are soft, add the tin of chopped tomatoes. Cook together briskly for 10 minutes with 1 tsp of red wine vinegar.

Add the drained broccoli, mixing the florets and rounds of stalk into the tomato sauce well and simmer gently for about 5 minutes, making sure the broccoli is not too al dente.

Serve in a dish with grated lemon rind and chopped fresh parsley atop.

Date and Coconut Cake

7 oz dates	1 tsp vanilla
1 tsp bicarbonate soda	6 oz soft brown sugar
9 fl oz warm water	6 oz plain flour
3 oz butter	1 tsp baking powder
1 egg	
9 inch cake tin	Oven heated to 180° C

Soak the dates in the warm water mixed with the bicarbonate soda for 10 minutes.

Add all the other ingredients and stir together vigorously. Pour into the lined tin (with protruding paper to lift cake out of tin or in loose bottomed tin) and bake for about 20 minutes.

Coconut topping

5 oz desiccated coconut	2 oz butter
3 oz muscovado sugar	3 tbsp milk

Put all the ingredients into a pan and heat gently to dissolve sugar. Increase heat and allow to come to a gentle simmer for 2-3 minutes.

Spoon mixture over the cake and return to the hot oven for about 10 minutes until golden.

Allow to cool in the tin.

There were plentiful aubergines at the market this morning so aubergines are on the menu. There is no hesitation about how to begin or pondering what to do with them. I suspect that our cook has a clutch of different ways to tantalise with aubergines.

The kitchen has only two high cupboards for the dry ingredients but, tardis like, a seeming infinite array of seeds, spices and basic ingredients appear out of them. But it is really no surprise that our cook is so at home in this confined cooking arena, that reminds me so much of a ship's galley, and would have most of us shrieking for more space. She began her working life cooking for 'film stars' on Mediterranean boats, so the apocryphal tale runs. Slim and purposeful, with a well-worn apron, perhaps an original, she works as if this room and its contents are extensions to her arms. She moves with balletic ease from trays, boards and knives to onions, spices and seeds; On tiptoe for high 'sweet' jars of flour and sugar, then a second later bent low for cream from the fridge without a hint of a groan or a sigh.

The aubergine dish takes shape.

Don't let's call them **stuffed** *aubergines she begs.*

Greek-style can't-we-call-them-something-other-than-stuffed Aubergines?
Serves 4

2 aubergines	*1 tsp brown sugar*
2 onions (red or white)	*1 red pepper (optional)*
2 cloves garlic	*1 lb lamb mince*
½ tsp cinnamon	*zest of a lemon*
2 tsp chopped fresh or 1 tsp dry thyme	*breadcrumbs*

Soak the aubergines whole in cold salted water for an hour. Pat them dry, stab them all over with a fork and grill, turning on all sides, until the flesh feels squidgy.

Split each aubergine in half from top to bottom.

Scoop out and chop up the flesh of the aubergine and keep on one side. Leave the aubergine shells in an oven dish or tin, waiting for the filling.

Cook the onions gently in a little olive oil with garlic, cinnamon, thyme, sugar. Add the red pepper diced if you have some. When the onion begins to change colour add the minced lamb and turn until brown and cooked through.

Add salt and pepper to taste. Mix in the chopped aubergine and grated zest of lemon.

Pile the mixture back into the aubergine shells.

Heat through in a medium oven and, just before serving, sprinkle with breadcrumbs, dot with butter and finish under the grill until sizzling and light brown.

But there are so many aubergines we need another recipe. Our cook has a great fondness for these chameleon vegetables that seem to change so much from one recipe to another.

Let's cross a few miles for the next.

Aubergine Sambal

Serves 4-6

2 medium aubergines	1 medium celeriac
1 tsp each turmeric, allspice, cumin and coriander seeds	2 cloves garlic
	Olive oil
1 tsp brown sugar	½ tin coconut milk
Pinch of chilli powder	Root ginger (shallot-sized)
1 small butternut squash	1 heaped tbsp desiccated coconut
2 sweet potatoes	Lemon zest

Cut the aubergines up into about 1 inch cubes and toss together with the spices, brown sugar and chilli powder.

Cut the remaining vegetables into similar sized cubes and parboil for 5-10 minutes until slightly soft.

Gently sweat the garlic, chopped or crushed, in some oil in a large pan and then add the aubergine cubes and fry briskly for about 10 minutes.

Add the drained parboiled vegetables to the aubergine, mixing together gently and continue cooking on a medium heat until soft. Add the coconut milk and the ginger, sliced thinly, and heat through thoroughly.

Serve sprinkled with toasted coconut, lemon zest and chopped coriander.

There is something that bothers me about the first of these recipes above.

The very word 'recipe' suggests an immutable and reliable guide for those who do not have the confident touch of our cook. But it is also important to remain true to the spirit of the style of cooking that our cook embodies.

I decide I must grapple with this contradiction head on.

If I write 'optional pepper' – that's going to throw some people. Don't people want to know what's best?

Our cook looks at me with astonishment. I think she might down tools on me. She works intuitively with food. She cooks by taste, inspiration and eye. She rarely measures or regards anything that she makes as fixed. So, as we go, we are having to pause frequently over the scales, pour out test quantities and remember, *remember* the temperature of the oven.

But this is a far deeper issue. Unwittingly I have opened up Pandora's jar.

Surely not! My recipes aren't for **beginners**!

Maybe I should censor the emphasis and the faint whiff of superiority. We can't offend the readers in chapter 2.

Cooking as an adventure into the unknown and unexpected is sacred to our cook. It is, after all, a religion I have, up to now, failed to take account of.

But she has an extraordinary instinct for blending flavours from her battery of herbs and spices and a creative flair for knowing which additions enhance and those which would sit oddly on the tongue. From where she stands it is hard for her to grasp that some of us, me in particular, might struggle to be sure, in the exciting new world of savoury and sweet combinations, whether putting chopped apricots in their cheese sauce could be one of those combinations that worked or not.

I am reminded of the time, a while back, when our cook looked at me with penetrating eyes and asked why anyone could possibly want, nay *need*, to open a jar of ready-sauce? Why, oh why, indeed? Because, to our cook, making a sauce is just a moment's more work than opening the jar. And how do you compare the quality? There is, we know, no comparison.

Oh no, dear cook, how ridiculous. I could never dream of opening a jar.

Garlic Chicken with Roast Pepper Purée

Serves 4

4 chicken breasts	*2 red + 2 yellow sweet peppers*
2 dsp dried thyme or 4 big sprigs fresh	*1 large onion*
1 tbsp white wine or balsamic vinegar	*4-6 large tomatoes*
1 tbsp runny honey	*1 dsp paprika*
1 tbsp olive oil	*Fresh parsley and rosemary*
3 fat cloves of garlic	*Oven heated to 180°C*

Mix together the thyme, vinegar, honey and oil with the chopped garlic ready for the marinade. Make a slit in the fat part of each chicken breast to form a pocket and coat all surfaces (inner and outer) with the marinade.

Place the chicken breasts in an oven proof dish and pour over any remaining marinade.

Cover with cling film for 30 minutes and leave to infuse.

Meanwhile chop the peppers, onion and tomatoes and sprinkle with paprika and olive oil in a roasting pan and roast for 30 minutes.

Remove from the oven and leave on one side to cool slightly, turning the oven down to 150°C ready for the chicken.

Using a draining spoon, remove the chicken from the marinade, and lightly seal both sides in a sparingly oiled, hot frying pan.

Add the marinade to the chicken and bring to the boil and return all to the oven dish.

Cover the dish with foil and bake in the oven for about 20 minutes. Test with something sharp to make sure the juices run clear and the meat is cooked through.

Meanwhile, process the peppers and tomatoes to make a purée, adding the marinade and juices from round the chicken.

Reheat / keep the purée hot in a pan on the stove and pour over the cooked chicken breasts.

Scatter with chopped parsley and rosemary to serve.

I think the score might just be one all though.

The other day our cook phoned me up after a fly-on-the-wall visit.

You remember that Mushroom tart recipe we did the other day.

Yes, of course.

Do you have it in your notes somewhere?

*Yes, of course. **I am** a writer.* I feel I am allowed a little superiority too.

There is relief in her voice as I remind her of some of the ingredients she must have decided to throw in on the hoof as she cooked it on my visit and couldn't now remember what they were. She needed to recreate the exact recipe as it had gone to an outlet beyond the Barn which wanted the *same* again.

It is important to realise that visitors to the Barn usually get unique variations on a recipe *theme*.

The next recipe is a vanguard. It served to demonstrate to our cook that, now and then, it can be useful to record a recipe for posterity.

Mushroom Croustade

Serves 6-8

1 medium onion

2 cloves garlic

Handful of fresh herbs

4 oz ground almonds

4 oz fresh breadcrumbs

6 oz softened butter

2 lb mushrooms

9-10 inch flan tin / dish

3 inch piece root ginger

Fresh coriander

Wine glass dry sherry

Small pot sour cream or crème fraiche

Orange zest

Handful toasted and chopped hazelnuts

Oven heated to 180°C

Chop the onion, garlic and herbs finely, then combine with the almonds and breadcrumbs. Work in the butter with the hands or a utensil, as preferred, until a sticky crumbly mixture is formed.

Pat this into the flan tin to form a base. Bake for about 15 minutes until the mixture holds together.

Gently simmer the sliced mushrooms in a pan with the ginger and the coriander stalks, both chopped.

When beginning to wilt and exuding their liquid add the sherry, and salt and pepper to taste. Bubble until the liquid is reduced.

Spread the mushrooms over the base and spoon the cream over this. Scatter with the chopped, toasted hazelnuts and orange zest.

Warm through in a medium oven and serve sprinkled with chopped coriander.

Chapter 3
Ruffled feathers

On this visit I shun my usual back entrance and turn the corner round the end of the barn and head towards the punters' entrance - a stable door, with upper section open wide, to let in a little air. Swallows bob and swing, nattering all the while, on overhead cables. The garden around the barn, with its rough-hewn rustic tables dotted about amongst low fruit trees, is still and waiting in the heat of the sun. The hotch potch of sawn timber, fence panels and old tyres live comfortably alongside a set of graceful sculptures. These tall angular shapes make me think of a clutch of women posing about and swishing skirted bottoms.

I hear a *sotto voce* crooning and sense a feathery movement out of the corner of my eye. A wire run, with four brown hens, sits newly on the edge of the garden where a notional boundary lies to separate the domain of those that live in the farmhouse from the to-ing and fro-ing at the Barn. I feel sure the hens weren't here on my last visit. The high stepping birds keek at me with beady eyes and sudden flicks of their heads.

 I think they know.

As I push through the stable door into the welcome cool of the Barn itself, I wonder if chicken will be on the menu today.

And it is.

Coq au Vin - Easy Style

Serves 4

4 chicken breasts	*2 sprigs rosemary or thyme (2 tsp dried)*
Seasoned flour	*4 large tomatoes*
2 onions	*1 large wine glass red wine*
2 large rashers streaky bacon	*1 tbsp tomato purée*
2 cloves of garlic	*16 black olives - dry or in oil (optional)*
4 oz mushrooms	*Fresh parsley*
1 tbsp brandy	*Oven heated to 180°C*

Cut the chicken breasts into thick strips and toss about in flour with salt and pepper added.

Chop the onions and garlic, slice up the bacon and cook all together in a frying pan, in a mix of oil and butter, until the onions are turning transparent.

Add the pieces of chicken, turning and browning them on all sides, increasing the heat as necessary.

Add the sliced mushrooms, rosemary or thyme, and brandy, and allow to bubble to reduce any excess liquid.

Transfer everything into an oven proof dish.

In the same frying pan cook the chopped tomatoes briskly until their liquid is reduced and thickened, pulling out any chunks of skin that come loose and seem in the way. Pour in the glass of red wine and bubble for another 3 minutes or so until thickened again.

Stir the tomato purée and the olives into the tomato sauce.

Add the tomato sauce to the chicken and bake in the oven uncovered for about 15 minutes until the chicken is tender.

Serve scattered with chopped fresh parsley.

The theme for this visit seems to have been set. Reality has to be confronted in many shapes and forms today. But first, let's face up to this struggle around growing animals and eating them. Everyone has their position. I have mine and the cook has hers.

I recall my recent delight at helping the cook gather a new and naïve bunch of hens out of the trees in her home garden at dusk, to stow them safely into their coop. The soft paradoxical weightlessness of these feathered creatures inspired a need in me to protect - not to gobble them up with relish.

But I so often do.

Could I wring a neck for the sake of food? I think I could, if hungry enough. But this distant possibility sits uneasily with my everyday acceptance that others do the deed, not always satisfactorily, in hidden sheds whilst I keep my hands clean. I am full of contradictions.

My compromise is that I eat meat sparingly and infrequently and I think our cook might work on similar principles. She seems to be keener to record her vegetarian recipes and since this is not purporting to be a vegetarian cookbook I have to nudge from time to time that some readers might want meat.

But let's be done with the chicken once and for all and go out with a grand and delicious flourish.

Stilton Chicken Pockets

Serves 6

6 chicken breasts *Chives if available*

1 wine glass of sherry *Zest of orange*

3-4 oz stilton cheese *12 rashers streaky bacon*

2 oz softened butter *Cornflour for thickening*

Fresh sage or dried if not available *Parsley*

Oven heated to 180°C

Remove the small appendage of meat on each chicken breast and save for another purpose (e.g. chicken goujons).

Leave the chicken breasts soaking in a good pour of sherry either overnight or for a few hours if possible.

Prepare the stilton and butter stuffing by mashing down the cheese and mixing together with the butter, chopped sage, chives and orange zest.

Slit into the side of the thickest part of each chicken breast with a sharp knife and spoon some stilton mixture into each 'pocket'.

Wrap 2 rashers of bacon around each stuffed breast, on the diagonal, to hold the 'pocket' together.

Lay out the chicken in an ovenproof dish.

Pour over the remains of the marinade and a slosh of extra sherry.

Cover firmly with foil and bake in the oven for 20 minutes.

Check the meat by stabbing and looking for clear-running juices.

Reduce the oven temperature to 130°C and continue cooking for 10 more minutes.

Check frequently enough to catch the chicken when it is just right and not over cooked.

Drain off the juices into a pan and thicken with cornflour. Add any leftover stilton mix to the sauce.

Pour this over the chicken pockets.

Scatter with chopped parsley and grated orange zest to serve.

The last of the chicken recipes.

This is a relief with the mood I'm in today. I'm more than ready for some vegetarian treats. And treats they are as the range and variety of vegetarian cooking, that flows from our cook's pots and oven, defy all the old stereotypes of vegetarian food being inextricably linked to unappetising dullness, worthiness and/or the ubiquitous pulse.

Here are two recipes without a bean in sight.

Asparagus Tart with olive oil pastry (with grateful thanks again to the hens)

Serves 6 to 8

Pastry

10 tbsp olive oil	*12 oz plain white flour*
2 tbsp water	*2 tsp salt*
3-4 cloves of garlic	*1 dsp chopped fresh rosemary*
12 inch flan tin	*Oven heated to 180°C*

Heat together the olive oil and water in a pan with the chopped garlic.

In a bowl, mix the flour, salt and rosemary.

Pour the hot oil mixture into the dry ingredients and mix quickly to a rough crumbly texture.

Tumble this into the greased flan tin and pat it round and up the sides to make a covering.

Lay 2 forks crosswise over the top (see page 14) and bake blind for 10-12 minutes until the pastry turns colour.

Filling

2 bundles of asparagus	*½ pint single cream*
3 egg yolks	*grated nutmeg*
2 whole eggs	*2-3 tbsp crunched hazelnuts and walnuts*
Turn oven down to 150°C	

Trim the asparagus and steam whole.

Arrange the asparagus in the part-baked tart case.

Mix the egg yolks together with whole eggs and with the cream. Add pinches of nutmeg, white pepper and salt and pour over the asparagus.

Cook in the oven until set.

Toast slightly crunched hazelnuts and walnuts together in a skillet and sprinkle on top of the tart to finish.

Just to contrast with the quintessentially homespun ingredients of the first recipe here is a variation on a dish our cook has drawn from more exotic locations.

Vegetable Tagine

Serves 6

3 medium onions	2 medium carrot
2 fat cloves garlic	2 medium potatoes
1 dsp each paprika, turmeric, ginger,	Vegetable stock
cinnamon and cumin	1 tin chopped tomatoes
1 lb butternut squash	Raisins
1 lb celeriac	Coriander
1 lb sweet potato	Chick peas (optional)

Chop the onion and garlic and cook gently in olive oil (mixed with vegetable oil if watching cost) in a largish pan, adding all of the spices until the flavours are blending and filling the air with their aromas.

Tumble in the cubed squash, celeriac, potatoes and carrot and mix well with the onion and spices and cook for 10 minutes with the lid on. Surround the vegetables with just enough vegetable stock to keep everything moist and add salt and pepper. Cook for another 10 minutes with the lid on.

Pour in the tin of tomatoes and cook briskly for 5 minutes and then reduce the heat and simmer until the vegetables are all soft but not falling apart.

Toss in a handful of raisins (cooked chickpeas could also be added at this point if a more substantial dish is wanted). Serve with chopped fresh coriander (and optional toasted coconut) sprinkled on top.

There are two guests in the Barn today. One has been coming to eat his lunch, once a week and every week, for the fourteen years that our cook has been here. The other guest is the postman who has decided to call back for a meal for the first time ever.

The postman definitely wants meat. So it's just as well our cook has also prepared a spicy lamb dish. She likes to give a choice.

From the way he doesn't hesitate one suspects his preference is probably for the red sort.

Iranian Style Lamb

Serves 6

1 lb butternut squash

8 oz ladies' fingers / okra

2 medium onions

2 fat cloves garlic

Seeds from 12 cardamom pods

2 lb boned shoulder of lamb

Oven heated to 180° C

Meat stock

Pinch grated nutmeg

8 oz dates soaked in Earl Grey tea

1 tbsp orange water

Fresh mint

Zest of an orange

Cut the butternut squash into rough 2 inch cubes. Dust them with flour and then roast in olive oil for about 20 minutes. Top and tail the ladies' fingers and cut them into diagonal chunks. Add these to the still-roasting squash for a further 10 minutes (30 minutes in total).

Chop the onion and garlic and cook gently with the cardamom seeds in a mix of olive oil and butter in a hob-to-oven casserole. Cut the meat into rough 2 inch cubes and then add to the onion and spice mix, turning up the heat to brown the lamb all over.

Surround with a small quantity of stock, nutmeg and seasoning. Cook for 1 hour in the oven, or on the stove, at a very low simmer, for a similar time. When the lamb is tender add the ladies' fingers, squash, the soaked dates puréed, and the orange water. Test for seasoning. Reheat through and serve with chopped mint and grated orange zest.

After the early morning start he has probably had, I think he will most likely need some hearty potatoes too.

Paprika Potato Wedges

1 lb potatoes	*1 tsp dried thyme*
2 oz butter	*Salt and ground pepper*
½ tsp paprika	*Oven heated to 180°C*

Parboil the potatoes, peeled and cut into wedges. Melt the butter in a roasting tin and add paprika, thyme, salt and ground pepper.
Coat the drained potato wedges in this mixture. Bake in the oven until brown, 20-30 minutes.

From my perch in the kitchen I can observe the two men sitting on separate, but close-by, tables. There is a little of the steady, pass-the-time-of-day talk between the two of them and our cook flits in and out as the food preparation allows, to add a little comment here and help find unanticipated crossings of paths to oil the flow of conversation. Our cook behaves towards them, not as her customers, but as her invited guests to whom she bears a social responsibility above and beyond the contract to provide them with food.

With her oft-returning 'guest' she has a rapport and an understanding of what he might wish for, born of years of experience. For a start, she knows that he will drink her homemade elderflower cordial - because he always does.

Elderflower Cordial

3 pints water	*40 elderflower heads (open and part open)*
2½ lb sugar	*3 lemons*
2 oz citric acid	

Dissolve the sugar in water in a large pan and bring slowly to the boil, stirring from time to time, and simmer for 3-4 minutes. Add the citric acid and lemon juice and immerse the elderflowers (well shaken to remove the bugs first). Leave to steep overnight. Sieve or strain the liquid into plastic or glass bottles (depending on storage) making sure you squeeze all the juice from the flower heads.
Freeze or keep in the fridge up to 3-4 weeks

I suspect she might also have a shrewd idea of what he will choose to eat but she carefully masks any clue of this. She keeps her professional distance. In this liberal establishment the diner has an *a priori* right to freedom of choice, without undue influence. On top of this our cook makes a strong commitment to all her dishes. It would not be her style to offer a sub-standard dish. How then to promote one over another? It is only ever a question of personal choice.

Today, I watch the parting minutes of the various guests and become aware that there is an uneasy ghost hovering over this final transaction at the end of the visit.

Money must change hands.

All the physical symbols of this unfortunate aspect of the last moments, after eating at the Barn, demote it. There is a grand vintage cash register set at one side of the front counter - entirely ornamental. It isn't clear it actually opens. Prices on the menu board are a little sketchy in places, or non-existent. Some figures are swiftly written down on a scrap of paper. A total is announced. The voice is robust, professional. However there is a wobble deep down.

It is unpleasant to bring money into this. Rude audacity to name amounts when what the Barn offers its guests is something without a price tag. Our cook would be much happier if she could exchange a skill with these people in some way. A tagine for some help with a crumbling fence or with a recalcitrant list of figures in her books. A tasty tart for the table or freezer is such an excellent barter in these other areas of her life.

But here at the Barn the relationship usually has to be different.

And today I can see our cook has her own internal struggle with it.

Just sometimes a meal can be offered in exchange for a basket of superfluous garden produce that is brought in by a customer. For our cook there is a simplicity and complete lack of tension in this kind of exchange. I can tell she would prefer it to be like this more often.

However this only works from time to time. And it doesn't really do away with the butcher's bill.

Our cook has to live and she must name her price.

Momentarily, reality has jaws and teeth. But the neck-wringing is swift. Money is handed over, change is found and the focus shifts quickly to rituals of leave-taking. Let's sweeten our taste before these visitors go.

Banana Date and Walnut Tart

1 quantity sweet pastry (see below)	4 egg whites
8 oz dates	9 oz sugar
4 bananas	1 tsp cornflour
3 oz walnuts	1 pinch cream of tartar
Small pot double cream	
Oven heated to 180°C	9-10 inch flan case

Line the flan case with pastry and bake blind with 2 forks across the base for 10 minutes in a hot oven.

Spread the base with chopped dates and lay bananas split long ways on top in a star shape.

Sprinkle the chopped walnuts in between the banana slices.

Pour over the double cream.

Whisk the egg whites with the sugar, cornflour and cream of tartar until thick.

Pile onto the flan and return to the oven, still at 180°C, for 5 minutes. Check for browning of the meringue topping.

Continue baking until the top is light brown all over and then turn down the oven to 100°C.

After 20 minutes more tap the meringue to see if it is crisp. If not, return to the oven for as many minutes as it takes.

Sweet Shortcrust Pastry

12 oz plain white flour	1 dsp sugar
6 oz white fat, margarine or butter	1 tsp water
1 large egg yolk or 2 small	

Work the fat into the flour to make a crumbly texture.

Add the sugar and bind together with the egg and water to make a roll-able dough.

Let it rest in the fridge for 30 minutes, if possible, before rolling out.

When baking blind a quick way of helping the pastry keep its shape in the tin is to lay 2 forks across the width of the base whilst it is cooked in the oven.

Chocolate Roulade

Serves 6-8

5 eggs	*Icing sugar and cocoa powder for dusting*
6 oz soft brown sugar	*½ pint double cream*
6 oz plain chocolate	*Caramelised hazelnuts*
3 tbsp water or liqueur of choice	*Handful fresh spearmint*
Heat oven to 200°C	*Greased and lined 10x14 inch Swiss roll tin*

Separate the egg yolks and whites into two bowls.

Whisk the yolks and sugar together until pale and thick.

Melt the chocolate in a bowl over simmering water. Add either the hot water or the liqueur and stir into the chocolate.

Beat the melted chocolate into the creamed egg and sugar quite energetically until smooth and even.

Whisk the egg whites until peaked and fold into the chocolate mixture.

Spread evenly in the tin and bake for about 12 minutes.

Turn the oven off, leave the door open, and allow to cool for 10 minutes.

Cover with a damp tea towel and leave for a further 10 minutes.

Turn out the sponge onto a similar sized tin, dish or board which has been liberally sprinkled with icing sugar and cocoa powder. Peel off the lining paper and allow to cool completely before spreading with thickly whipped cream with added chopped spearmint and caramelised hazelnuts.

Roll and enjoy!

Caramelised Nuts

2 oz butter	*1 tbsp water*
2 oz brown sugar	*6 oz chopped hazelnuts (or other / mixed nuts)*

Melt together the butter, sugar and water in a saucepan. Boil rapidly for about 3 minutes until dark brown.

Add the chopped nuts and swirl around until well coated. Leave to cool and then use as desired, storing any excess in an airtight jar for a later occasion.

My visit to the Barn today has been quite demanding. I'm not sure I bargained for all the emotional consequences of being a fly-on-the-wall.

The sun is strong on the way home and I feel my energies are a little frayed and sapped. I have transcribed some cooling and restorative soups recommended for this kind of occasion.

Just the time to try them out.

Fresh Tomato Soup (Thai-style perhaps)

2 lbs tomatoes (the redder and riper the better)
1 dsp mild curry powder
1 tsp dark brown sugar   *handful fresh coriander*
1 tbsp dark soy sauce   *1 tin coconut milk*
1 tbsp lemon juice   *cumin seeds*
Pinch chilli powder   *lime zest*

Chop the tomatoes and simmer in a large pan on a low heat until they are going soft. Add the curry powder, brown sugar, soy sauce, lemon juice, chopped coriander stalks, chilli powder and cook together for 10 minutes. Stir in the coconut milk and liquidise. Adjust seasoning. Serve chilled (or hot) with a scattering of toasted coconut, chopped coriander leaves and lime zest.

Cucumber Soup

1 large cucumber   *2 tsp olive oil*
½ pint yoghurt   *2 tsp white wine vinegar*
5 oz single cream   *2 oz walnuts*
1 crushed garlic clove   *butter*
Handful fresh mint

Peel and chop the cucumber leaving it, sprinkled with salt, for about 30 minutes to drain.
Rinse, then add to the rest of the ingredients. Put all the other ingredients in a processor with two thirds of the cucumber.
Whizz until smooth, adding salt and pepper to taste. Add the remaining cucumber to the soup and chill.
Serve sprinkled with chopped walnuts that have been tossed in a hot pan with melted butter.

Chapter 4
From a boat to a barn

We all know that no two people, cooking to an identical recipe, ever produce quite the same dish. The flavours, textures, visual appearance seem to take on their own unique variation. An unscientific alchemy goes on that leaves those of us who struggle with the art of cooking baffled.

'It is foolproof,' we are assured by our more gifted cooking friend or colleague. But alas, in spite of painstaking measuring and sourcing of ingredients, the product of our efforts is just not the same. We become sullenly convinced they are withholding some crucial element or process to ensure our inferior result. We juggle cooking temperatures and herbs and spices hoping to discover what has been missing. Often we are disappointed.

The ferocious competition for the best sponge cake at village flower shows, up and down the country over several generations, has only been kept alive because of this mysterious variability.

Given that weighing scales and oven temperatures are moderately reliable the element which is most slippery in this extraordinary phenomenon is the personality of the cook. This can only be described as a kind of magic because it is hard to grasp why someone's character should give rise to the rainbow of differences between the dishes that come out of the oven or pan.

So, it would seem our cook's early formative life could be as important an ingredient in the food she creates as is the atmosphere of the Barn itself.

Anyway, I am sure we are all curious to know a bit about her origins and how she came to be where she is today.

Our cook demurs at first. She is not sure people will really want to read about her own history. A little pressure is needed to convince her that it will be both welcomed by a reader and relevant to the story.

It is best told in her own words.

46

At home, when growing up, the meat served at Sunday lunches was distinguishable only by the presence of: a) Mint sauce or b) horseradish. Otherwise one was simply staring at slices of dark brown leather. I must soften this condemnation of my mother's lack of passion in the kitchen by telling you that the one dish she did make with any vestige of taste was this:

Ingredients for Mum's Savoury Meat Patties

8 oz minced pork
8 oz pork sausage meat
1 packet sage and onion stuffing
1 large onion
1 beaten egg

The onion was roughly chopped and boiled. When soft in went enough of the Paxo stuffing to absorb the liquid (not forgetting how much it swells), followed by the meats and the egg – all suitably combined. (I'm trying very hard at this point not to say 'Add a pinch of nutmeg, a good twist of black pepper, a soupçon of –' no, no, no. This is my mother's recipe and I shall not tamper with it.) Work into patty shapes and toss in flour (Did she add salt and pepper? You could add a pinch of celery seeds – no, be quiet!) Fry the patties in shallow oil for about 10 minutes on each side over a brisk heat. The outside should be crunchy and the inside moist and – yes, very tasty!

Not having a particularly warm and loving home life, I scampered off to France at seventeen (having been au pair to my French teacher's pen friend in Corsica the summer before and loved it).

I hitched down the Route Napoleon and eventually fetched up in Cannes.

I did any odd job: washing cars, scrubbing decks, until one day I was asked to see a skipper on a beautiful yacht called Delia.

Unbeknownst to me the captain had asked his crew member to find 'some innocent' to clean the engine room. The job title had not been mentioned to me.

The Captain glowered at my arrival, not least because I had stomped on board during his siesta. However he suggested I cook lunch for him and Bernie, the roguish deckhand, the next day, for the princely sum of 5 francs, being their daily food allowance (a bit like having £2 per person per day in today's currency). If I was really worth my salt, I could manage to stretch the food far enough to allow a crumb or three to fall on my own plate.

I set off the next day from my hostel and happened upon the Charcuterie Lyonnaise – an exotic emporium of deliciousness where I wandered and pondered over ready-made dishes that might please my 'sailors' and eventually made my purchases.

Of course, I rearranged the food into the boat's own crockery and was soon regarded with a certain respect that so much could be provided with so little finance. How did she do it? Simple. She was cashing in her travellers cheques and bathing in compliments. Keeping face was paramount.

The following two dishes were particularly popular and I eventually learned how to produce them myself. There's really not much cooking involved.

Sweet Pepper with Goat's Cheese and Anchovy

Serves 4 as a starter with mixed leaf salad surrounding each half pepper.

2 red or yellow sweet peppers	*Chilli powder*
4 spoonfuls goat's cheese	*Zest of lemon*
4 anchovies in olive oil	*Fresh basil*

Put the whole peppers under a hot grill, turning and allowing the skin to shrivel and blacken.

Rub to remove most of the skin and pull out the stalk. Cut the peppers in half and remove the seeds.

Place a spoonful of goat's cheese, mixed with a chopped anchovy, pinch of chilli powder, zest of a lemon and chopped basil, in each half.

Put under the grill until the cheese is melted and bubbling.

Stuffed Avocado

Half an avocado per person or a whole one if small.

Small quantity ratatouille

Lemon juice and zest

Breadcrumbs

Black olives

Fresh herbs

Remove the flesh from the avocadoes and chop roughly. Mix with an equal quantity of ratatouille with an added splash of lemon juice.

Heap back into the skins and sprinkle with breadcrumbs and heat under a medium grill.

Sprinkle with some chopped black olives and fresh herbs.

However, eventually, as in most cases of slightly dodgy doings, it all fell apart.

I was emerging from the Charcuterie laden with goodies when I bumped, literally, into 'my captain'. Rats! My gaffe was blown.

A frown, then a bemused smile crossed his face and without a word he picked up the, by now broken, baguette, took my elbow firmly and led me about two hundred metres up the hill and, still mute, indicated the vast area of the Marché Forvil. This is one of the biggest and best produce markets on the south coast. I could only stand open-mouthed and gaze at stall upon stall of vegetables, fruit, cheese, meat, fish. It was a life changing moment. I was suddenly head over heels in love with food.

I was stunned and thrilled by the colour, the variety of shapes and textures on the heaped up stalls and the wonderful smells that assailed my nostrils. Three simple recipes spring to mind which epitomise the richness of this Mediterranean initiation.

Aubergine Frittata

Serves 4 as a starter

2 aubergines	1 tbsp cream
4 egg yolks	1 tbsp of chopped parsley mixed with any herb of choice
1 clove garlic	

Slice the aubergines into rounds. Soak in salted water for 30 minutes. Drain and pat dry.

Drizzle with oil and place under a hot grill until golden and then turn and toast the other side with more drizzles of oil.

Lift onto absorbent paper.

Separate the egg yolks into a bowl, whisk them together with the cream, herbs, crushed garlic and salt and pepper.

Heat a frying pan and add the aubergine rounds until they start to sizzle. Pour over the egg mix and allow to set on the bottom.

Then put the pan (but not its handle) under a medium to hot grill until the top is puffy and golden.

Serve with salad leaves dressed in a mustardy vinaigrette.

Open Spinach Tart

Half a quantity of shortcrust pastry (see page 14) to which has been added: a handful of chopped walnuts and chopped fresh sage and a twist of black pepper, with the dry ingredients.

1½ lb spinach

6 oz fromage frais

2 egg yolks

½ tsp grated nutmeg

9 inch flan tin or dish

Salt and pepper

1 red and 1 yellow sweet pepper

Fresh basil

Oven heated to 180°C then 160°C

Line the flan tin with pastry and bake the pastry blind for 10 minutes with forks on top.

Lightly steam the spinach in a very small quantity of water until just wilted.

Drain it thoroughly and chop.

Whisk the eggs, fromage frais, salt, pepper and nutmeg together.

Add the spinach to the egg mix and tip the combined ingredients into the pastry case.

Bake at 160°C until set.

Roast the peppers, cut out the seeds and slice into strips. Lay these over the top of the tart.

Finally strew chopped fresh basil over the layer of pepper strips.

Fennel in Orange

Slice and chop 3 or 4 heads of fennel and with 8 whole garlic cloves fry them in a little olive oil.

Cover the frying pan with a lid.

When the fennel has softened and is tinged with brown pour on some orange juice to cover the base and toss in a handful of fennel seeds. Cover again and braise the fennel until soft. Taste for salt and add if wished.

Transfer to an oven dish, sprinkle the top with breadcrumbs, sesame and sunflower seeds and cuts of butter.

Flash under the grill to toast but not singe the seeds. Serve with grated orange zest and generous chopped flat-leafed parsley.

I worked as stewardess on a 70 metre yacht that summer and eventually paired up with Delia's captain to cook for the great but not always so good, on our own yacht, the Pirate Princess, which we purchased unseen, as it lay on the sea bed having sunk off Antibes.

My 'amour' (he was much too old to call a boyfriend: 32, divorced, 2 children) worked on renovating the boat while I secured an all important paying job ashore, with a naval architect, as a bi-lingual secretary.

I had been assured that the boat rescue was a good business proposition as the engines should be undamaged, in spite of their dousing, and were well worth the few hundred pounds we paid for the whole thing. This was a very long time ago. So we worked hard and returned her to her former glory and chartered her out, with ourselves as skipper and cook, for a couple of years.

This was in the late sixties and we had an eclectic mix of guests. One of our charters slides into my mind. We were procured by a delightful elderly gentleman who belonged to a well-known cognac distilling dynasty and who was clearly obliged to sample the amber nectar on a regular basis lest it fall short of perfection. Anyway, we had dropped anchor in a secluded little bay in Corsica when he challenged the crew and his guests to a game of boules on the beach. Everyone disappeared below to collect swimming costumes, sun cream etc. As I clambered up the stairs from our fo'c'sle cabin I was just in time to see said gent pick up the briefcase-shaped bag full of boules and plunge over the side of the boat!

I do not need, I suspect, to point out at this juncture that a metal boule weighs over a pound and the bag would have contained at least twelve of them. Our gent disappeared from sight under the water, with terrifying speed, only to reappear seconds later, minus the boules, with a look on his face that I can only describe as a mix of indignation and bafflement that this should have happened.

A great deal of laughter ensued as no harm was done, boules retrieved, all hoisted into the dinghy, and crew and guests at last reached the beach to enjoy their game.

The cove was only accessible from the sea and soon a small fishing boat was pushed up on the beach by her skipper, a wizened, nut-brown Corsican thrusting a huge bucket of freshly caught calamari at us. Supper for that night naturellement.

Corsican Calamari

Serves 4

2 lbs calamari	*Pinch of chilli powder*
2 medium onions	*6 large tomatoes (or tin of chopped tomatoes)*
2 fat cloves garlic	*Wine glass of white wine*
2 tsp thyme	*Black olives*
2 tsp chopped parsley	*Grated lemon*

Given the luxury of choice, pick small calamari, cut the main body away from the tentacles and wash everything thoroughly to remove all the ink. Cut tentacles into cubes ready.

In a deep frying pan or shallow saucepan, cook the chopped onions and garlic in olive oil until lightly coloured.

Add the herbs, chilli, chopped tomatoes. Swish around to combine and pour on the glass of white wine.

Put on a lid and allow to cook down for about 15 minutes.

In another pan heat the olive oil to fry all the cubes of calamari quickly on both sides.

Add these to the tomato mixture, some black olives as wished, plus grated lemon, and heat gently together for about 10 minutes.

Serve with rice.

For a more exaggerated lemony taste add chopped lemongrass to the tomato sauce at the same time as the herbs.

Of course, the availability of fish meant the cooking on board the Pirate Princess often had a fishy bent so here is an unusual first course on this theme.

Plaice with Banana and Almond

Serves 4

4 plaice

Flour for rolling	*2 large lemons*
Egg for rolling	*Parsley*
Seasoned breadcrumbs	*Butter*
2-3 bananas depending on size	*Oil*
3 oz flaked almonds	*Paprika*

Skin and cut each plaice into 6 strips (goujons).

Roll the goujons of plaice in flour, then in the beaten egg followed by the seasoned breadcrumbs. Heat a mix of oil and butter in a frying pan and fry small batches of goujons briskly for a minute or two on each side without the pieces of fish touching each other.

Pop each batch into a warm oven whilst you finish the whole quantity.

Wipe out the pan and add a knob of butter. Cut the bananas so that you have 24 slices (one slice for each goujon) and cook on each side in the butter until golden. Add to the fish.

Return the pan to the heat with just enough butter to grease and toss in the almonds, stirring them about until coloured. Add these to the fish and bananas.

Remove some zest from the lemons and keep on one side. Squeeze the juice from the lemons, pour into the pan and season, heating gently.

Arrange 6 goujons, 6 slices of banana, a sprinkle of almonds on each plate, top with chopped parsley, lemon zest, a dusting of paprika and a pour of lemon juice.

The adage that a boat is a hole into which money is constantly poured is indeed a truism and, after a couple more years of going it alone, we finally sold the Pirate Princess and worked on far richer people's vessels.

One learned to be very innovative when setting off for, say Sardinia, with six guests and three crew, without putting into any sizeable port for three weeks. Victualling up was - tricky.

Once there were two days remaining before the final port of a charter with nowt in the larder but: bread, olive oil, onion, garlic, bacon, cabbage, milk and eggs. The punters were, however, catching a fair amount of fish.

Breakfast was pain perdu replacing butter with oil. Lunch, squares of bread fried up on onion and garlic and any available fish. Dinner, a layered pudding of bread, bacon, cabbage, with eggs and milk sloshed over, and slowly baked until crusty and golden.

It must be pointed out that I had plenty of herbs and spices and also, don't forget, the duty-free wines and spirits. Those two days, it has to be said, passed in a glow of alcohol and a total acceptance of the rigours of life at sea.

To compensate for a certain amount of improvisation in the main courses I became adept at finishing a meal with a bit of a flourish. This was often in the form of a Grand Marnier soufflé. Eggs and alcohol, you see, a real win-win combination and, in spite of their reputation, a soufflé is virtually impossible to fail at as long as you whip up the whites thoroughly, pop it into a very hot oven and don't overcook it.

However, I did begin to wonder whether I had over-egged the pudding when I heard myself referred to as the 'queen of soufflés' by the end of the charter.

Grand Marnier Soufflé

Serves 4-6

4 egg yolks	*6 egg whites*
2 tbsp caster sugar	*¼ tsp cream of tartar*
2 tbsp Grand Marnier	
Heat oven to 200°C	*7 inch straight sided oven dish, buttered and dusted with icing sugar*

Put the yolks and sugar in a bowl over a pan of simmering water and beat until thick and they start to hold shape ('ribbons' in the mixture).

Add the Grand Marnier and then remove the bowl from the heat and dunk into a shallow dish of cold water to cool the mixture.

Beat the egg whites vigorously with the cream of tartar until stiff. Quickly fold in the yolk and sugar mix and then tip straight into the oven dish.

Bake for 12-15 minutes in the middle of the oven until set and golden.

Serve with sliced fresh oranges sprinkled with Grand Marnier and with Langue de Chat biscuits.

Chapter 5
Friends

On one of my visits, the whole of rural East Suffolk seems to be suffering an over-indulgence of flies. A mysterious test of everyone's ability to suppress irritation and revulsion and accept inevitability as well as infinity. Just another piece, after all, in the circle of life.

It gives me a timely reminder of my status.

As a fly-on-the wall one of my limitations is a pitifully short life span. Not being around for long is a definite disadvantage for my task here. But what about for the fly?

I feel I must give some credit where credit is due, even though I might upset a few readers who find these creatures too abhorrent to be considered in a space where there is also food. I just wish to raise a note of sympathy for a persecuted kind: if it were not for flies' mercifully short clinging to this mortal coil, if they chose to make full use of those sticky feet and resist, just imagine the pile up.

However, for me, one brief summer of hanging around in corners and watching out for spiders, is not enough to grasp the length and breadth of the Barn's unfolding over a decade and a half. I need to talk to those who know.

There is a clutch of customers - but no, they might have to be called friends, at least some of the time, who have been coming to the barn since forever. Or so it seems to them. Time before the Barn is so dim and distant and the possibility of time without the Barn is like an anchovy without salt.

This chapter, dedicated to the loyalty of these customers who have played such an important part in sustaining the life of this out-of-the-way eating place, will be interspersed with recipes without rhyme, reason or particular preamble. Just a record of some of the most asked for and firm favourites of these people and many others.

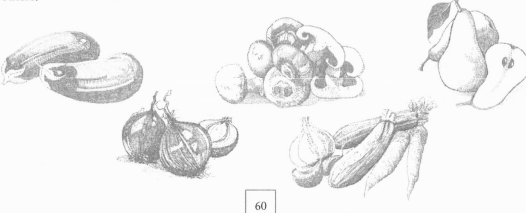

Tunisian Citrus Pudding

The Cake

2 oz breadcrumbs (white or wholemeal)	*1½ tsp baking powder*
4 oz ground almonds	*4 eggs*
6 oz sugar	*5 fl oz sunflower oil*
Zest of an orange	*Toasted flaked almonds*
Zest of a lemon	
Cold oven	*9 inch cake tin*

Combine all the ingredients in a bowl, apart from the oil. Then, using a whisk, add the oil little by little whisking well in between each addition. Only add the oil to the point where you have a thick (pancake) batter.

Pour into a greased and lined tin and place in a cold oven. Turn the heat up to 190° C and leave for about 30 minutes. Open the oven door carefully and check how well it is cooked. Shake a little. If the pudding still wobbles allow it to cook for a few more minutes.

When finally it seems set insert a skewer to make sure it comes out cleanly.

Remove the pudding from the oven and allow to cool for a minute or two. Turn it out of its tin and place on a plate the right way up and pour over the syrup (see below). Sprinkle with toasted almonds.

Citrus Syrup

Juice of an orange	*3 oz sugar*
Juice of a lemon	*Cloves, cinnamon, ginger according to taste*

While the pudding is baking boil juice, spices and sugar together briskly for a few minutes until reduced and syrupy. Leave to one side until the pudding is ready for the syrup.

Several of the most longstanding and regular visitors to the Barn that speak to me have kept the unshakeable belief that, if they were not actually the very first people to walk through the door on the first day it swung open, they were surely only an antenna's breadth away from being them.

Imam Bayildi (The Priest Swooned)

An Imam is reputed to have fainted when he tasted this Turkish dish.

Serves 4

2 aubergines	*1 dsp chopped fresh or dried thyme*
2 red onions	*Handful raisins (or dried fruit)*
Olive oil	*1 tin chopped tomatoes*
2 cloves garlic	*2 tbsp pine nuts*
1 tsp brown sugar	*Sprigs of fresh mint*
1 tsp cinnamon	*lemon zest*

Soak the aubergines in cold salted water for 30 minutes. Stab the skins all over. Place in a baking tin or dish under a medium grill, checking them and turning from time to time until they are squidgy to touch.

Chop the onions finely and sweat gently in olive oil in a frying pan until starting to soften. Add the chopped garlic, sugar, cinnamon, thyme and raisins. Stir and cook until the onions are fully soft. Pour in the tomatoes and add salt and pepper as wished. Simmer for 10 minutes or so to thicken.

When the aubergines can be handled without burning the fingers, slice them in half and scoop out most of the flesh leaving a layer next to the skin. Leave the skins in the baking tin.

Chop the scooped aubergine flesh and add to the tomato and onions. Mix and taste for flavouring.

Pile the mixture back into the aubergine skins. Sprinkle the stuffed aubergines with pine nuts and lightly toast under the grill. Serve with chopped fresh mint and grated lemon zest.

These people find it hard to say in just a few words why the Barn has been somewhere they have kept coming back to again and again over so many years. They have difficulty 'summing it up', need time to think, want to write it down or are prepared to invest quite a long time trying to get across what has captured them as a loyal customer.

I wonder if I am being a nuisance. Am I asking for the impossible?

They do not leave me feeling so. Trying to put into words what they have found to be special about the Barn seems to be an effort worth making; especially if it gives something back to the cook

They are not the only ones who want to do this, our cook has hundreds of individual 'thank you' notes for meals at the Barn. The kind of notes we ourselves might only expect to receive from close friends to whom we had given something extra special.

How does the Barn qualify for this accolade? Or is it just that people in this part of Suffolk are exceptionally well brought up when it comes to their ps and qs?

Pear Frangipane

Quantity of sweet shortcrust pastry (see page 42)

4 oz sugar	*1 tsp almond essence*
4 oz butter	*3-4 ripe pears*
1 egg	*Toasted almonds*
4 oz ground almonds	*Lemon zest*
1 tbsp cornflour	
8-10 inch flan tin	*Oven heated to 180°C*

Line the flan tin with pastry and bake blind with forks laid across for about 10 minutes until turning colour.
Beat together the sugar and the butter. Gradually add the egg, pour by pour, alternating with spoons of ground almonds mixed with the cornflour combining well as you go. Stir in the almond essence. Spread the mixture over the pastry base. Peel and slice the pears and arrange them overlapping on top of the almond mixture.
Bake in the oven for about 30 minutes until the almond base is light brown and set.
Sprinkle with toasted almonds and lemon zest.

So when I ask for some help to understand why the barn has kept its faithful following, these long-time customers suggest that the Barn has offered them something unique over the years that they have not found anywhere else.

At first it seems most important to tell me what the Barn *isn't*. It *isn't* one of the formulaic eating places that are two-a-penny elsewhere. Both the up-market and the down-market kind. It isn't image-conscious and it certainly doesn't give any impression of commercial self-interest.

As the conversation continues I notice that the Barn is described in rather a strange way. There are many aspects to it that, in the cold light of day, could be off-putting to some customers. However this might seem to an outsider, for these insiders the Barn satisfies a very individual, perhaps even idiosyncratic, wish-list. It's certainly not what everyone would be looking for in an eating place. In part it's the Barn's robust imperfections that have attracted and held these friends; its total disregard of trends, style and need to project an image.

Yet there *is* an image of the Barn that these longstanding patrons hold in their minds' eye, even if some might call it idealised. The resilience of this image seems to lie in the fact that the relationship they have developed over time with this eating place is a deeply personal one.

And this is why these people must be called 'friends'.

Bobotie

Serves 6

4 onions	*4 oz old bread*
2 large tart apples	*3-4 fl oz milk*
1 dsp curry powder	*3 eggs*
1 dsp oregano or marjoram	*8 bay leaves*
2 lb beef mince	*Sesame seeds*
1 dsp balsamic vinegar	*Parsley*
1 dsp dark brown sugar	*Lime leaves or zest of lemon*
6 oz dates and dried apricots	
Zest of large lemon	*Oven heated to 150°C*

Chop the onions and apples finely and gently cook in a pan in butter and oil. As they start to soften add the curry powder, oregano and salt and pepper.

Raise heat a little and add the mince, mixing and stirring until the meat is browned - about 10 minutes.

Add the vinegar and sugar.

Chop the dates and apricots and add to the meat with the grated zest of the lemon.

In a bowl, soak the bread in the milk, until it is soft and squidgy. Scrunch out excess milk and add the soaked bread to the meat. Stir to blend through the mixture.

Spread the meat into a greased ovenproof dish. Mix the eggs and milk (squeezed out of the bread) together and pour over the whole dish. Poke bay leaves into the mixture at intervals. Bake for about 30 minutes until set.

Serve cut into sections with sprinkles of chopped parsley, chopped lime leaves (you can buy jars of these in many shops but if you cannot find them more grated lemon zest is fine) and toasted sesame seeds.

The Barn that the friends conjure up is eternally rustic; unpretentious and unpolished in every sense of the word; it has rickety chairs and not always quite enough heating.

They are very truthful. None of this has escaped their notice.

It is remote and out of the way of the mainstream world. It doesn't quite belong in the 20th Century let alone the 21st.

And yet it is accessible, also in every sense of the word; not so very far from a main road, if you know it is there; it welcomes you, enfolds you and offers you an experience that is more satisfying than just the food that fills your stomach.

This is what they tell me.

And this is what they love:

The posies of flowers on the tables, the real linen napkins, nothing matching - including the napkins, the irregular 'cut' of butter in a small dish, the homemade bread that comes with the meal, the music, the art on the walls, the simplicity, lack of frippery and unnecessary fuss in all the furnishing and décor. All the indications that husbandry of resources is an abiding principle of the house.

And they haven't even begun on the food, let alone the cook herself.

Bread

3 lb flour (any mix of wholemeal, spelt, rye and white flours - organic by preference)

2 sachets dried yeast	*Salt and pepper*
1 ¼ pint warm water	*1 dsp black treacle*
2 tbsp olive oil	*3-4 medium loaf tins*

Additions and variations:

1. Chopped sage leaves and walnuts   *4. Cinnamon and sunflower seeds*

2. Parsley, garlic and olives   *5. Pumpkin seeds and cardamom seeds*

3. Sun dried tomatoes and basil

Use approximately 3 tbsp of any of these additives when combined.

Place the flour, yeast and additions of choice, with some salt and pepper, in a large bowl.

Add treacle to the warm water and have ready nearby.

Pour the olive oil onto the flour mixture, followed by the water added slowly, mixing the while with a sturdy fork or wooden spoon.

Continue to add liquid and mix (use hands if that becomes easier) until you have a soft, pliable lump of dough. Add more warm water if necessary to achieve this.

Knead and stretch the dough for at least 5 minutes until the dough is elastic, remembering that, when using wholemeal flour, the dough will not become as elastic as with white flour however much it is kneaded.

Warm and grease the loaf tins and divide the dough between them, half filling each tin.

Cover with a plastic bag and leave in a warm place until well risen in the tin.

Heat the oven to 200°C and bake the loaves for 35-40 minutes.

Remove the bread from their tins for the last 5 minutes and then tap on their bases to be sure there is a hollow sound to say they are done. Cool on a rack.

The food, they say, is full of unexpected flavours, an adventure for the taste buds, satisfying and plentiful. There is variety and unpredictability but also reliability in the standards of the meals. There is a huge willingness to be accommodating to special diets, foibles and even children.

Treacle Tart

One quantity sweet shortcrust pastry (see page 42)
8 oz sweet scones or cake or tea bread – that everyone has tired of

Golden syrup	*1 dsp mixed spice*
1 dsp lemon juice	*Desiccated coconut*
10 inch flan tin	*Oven heated to 180°C*

Line the tin with pastry and bake base blind for 10 minutes using 2 forks laid across the base to retain the shape of the case.

In a bowl, crumble the scone/cake/loaf with the mixed spice and gradually pour in the syrup and mix gently until the crumbs are soaked.

Mix in the lemon juice until the ingredients stick together and then spread into the pastry case.

Sprinkle with lightly toasted desiccated coconut.

But above all, of course, is that indefinable something that our cook herself brings to the Barn.

The longstanding friends *try* to define it. They are determined to give it everything they can without resorting to hyperbole, thereby cheapening the effect. I'm not sure I can do them justice.

Let it just be said that our cook offers an unusual welcome that makes the people who visit feel special, unique and entirely 'at home'. The dimension this brings to the food eaten here is without adequate description but keeps people coming back for more.

Our cook will want to turn the tables, I know, and offer her thanks to all those friends who have made the life of the Barn *so* alive. A cook is nothing without people to eat and enjoy her food.

The friends tell me firmly that the pleasure is all theirs.

Aubergine Provencal

Serves 4

4 aubergines	*1 tsp red wine vinegar*
4 medium onions	*Zest of a lemon*
2 sticks of celery	*4 oz emmental and parmesan mixed*
3 fat cloves of garlic	*Handful breadcrumbs*
8 large ripe tomatoes	*Chopped fresh herbs*
(or a tin of chopped tomatoes)	*Olive oil and butter*

1 dsp herbs (mix of marjoram, oregano and basil works well)

Medium rectangular oven proof dish

Slice the aubergines and leave in cold salty water for about 30 minutes. Some people think this is unnecessary but I find it 'plumps' them up when you grill them.

Lay them out in a tin and drizzle with olive oil. Place under a medium grill and cook on both sides until golden.

Meanwhile chop the onions, celery, garlic and cook gently in a mix of butter and oil for about 10 minutes.

Add the tomatoes, herbs, wine vinegar and seasoning and cook until a delicious unctuous consistency is achieved.

Alternate the aubergine slices, sprinkled with lemon zest, and the tomato sauce in layers. Finish with a layer of aubergine.

Spread the breadcrumbs and grated cheese as the final layer and finish off under the grill until golden brown.

Serve with a sprinkling of fresh chopped herbs.

Chapter 6
This voyage ends

This final chapter opens with the flavour of, if not sadness, then certainly regret, in the air. Our cook feels we need some sustaining food to see us through and the chapter is woven with her selection.

Spicy Cauliflower Soup

Serves 4

1 cauliflower	*1 onion*
1 tsp coriander seeds	*2 cloves garlic*
½ tsp cumin seeds	*½ tsp salt*
½ tsp black pepper	*½-1 lemon*
½ tsp turmeric	*Vegetable stock*

Pound the seeds in a pestle and mortar briefly. Then, in a suitably sized saucepan, fry all of the spices in butter for a couple of minutes.

Add the onion and cloves of garlic, chopped finely, and a small pour of oil and cook gently for 2 or 3 minutes.

Tumble in the cauliflower, broken into florets, and mix around adding enough stock to cover the vegetables by about two inches. Add salt and simmer until soft.

Whizz in a blender to a smooth consistency and add juice from ½-1 lemon according to taste. Reheat the soup, adding more stock if too thick.

Serve scattered with flaked almonds that have been tossed in hot butter with added paprika, sesame and poppy seeds.

After a baking autumn, when the hot sun has lingered on through the waning days as if determined to make the most of its limited presence, the wind has changed. Cold easterlies are nuzzling at the external crevices of the old building and their eddies creep inexorably inside. They work much too hard. How cruel they are. Small chills begin to waft to and fro amongst the welcoming warmth of the Barn. People who might be bothered by this arrive now with an extra layer or pullover discretely tucked under their arm, just in case. It doesn't stop them coming.

Lamb Tagine

Serves 6

2 large onions

3 cloves garlic

1½ lb leg of lamb

Olive oil

1 dsp each paprika, cinnamon, ginger

1 tsp each allspice, nutmeg, cumin

Meat stock

6 oz prunes or apricots

1 tbsp chopped preserved lemon (optional)

Oven heated to 130°C

Finely chop the onions and garlic.

Cut the lamb into rough 2 inch cubes.

In a bowl, combine the spices, together with a pour of olive oil.

Coat the lamb in this mixture and leave together with the onions and garlic overnight or for a few hours to steep.

In a hot frying pan, brown the meat briskly on all sides in batches and transfer to a hob-to-oven casserole, with the onions and garlic.

Barely cover the meat with stock and bring to the boil, then turn the heat down to a gentle simmer. Add the prunes or apricots.

Cook in the oven for about 1 hour with the casserole lid on.

This dish improves if left to go cold. It is possible then to remove unwanted fat that will have floated to the top.

Reheat for later consumption - possibly the next day. Check and add seasoning before serving.

If liked or available, serve with preserved lemons (see recipe below). Either add the chopped lemon to the tagine before serving or hand round separately in a small dish.

Tagine goes well with couscous and roasted butternut squash and carrots with added cardamom and orange zest.

Preserved Lemons

Take a normal ½ to ¾ lb jam jar and sterilise it. Have 6 lemons and 4 tablespoons of salt at the ready.

Cut the lemons into quarters and start to layer these into the jar, alternating with a generous covering of salt.

Press each layer down firmly.

Put a circle of greaseproof paper in the lid of the jar and screw on. Give the jar a good shake and leave in a cool room.

Next day you will find the lemons have softened and shrunk down a little and you may be able to add another layer of quartered lemons and salt.

When you cannot squeeze any more into the jar leave it sealed in a cool room for four weeks.

Give the jar an occasional shake.

At the end of this time your lemons are 'preserved' and ready to use.

Once opened, keep the jar in the fridge.

The customers have continued to flow in all through the warm days and on into the end-of-season weeks when winter is lurking somewhere not far across the fields.

It has been satisfyingly busy.

Normally our cook prepares to take a well-earned break during the lowest months of winter, re-gathering her forces to fling open her doors again, ready for the birds' spring, their and our wooing time, in mid February.

This year is not like other years.

There is change in the air and an end of an era.

The doors of the Barn close for the last time in December - not to re-open.

Quince and Apple Crumble

Serves 6

1½ lb apple	*6 oz oats*
1 lb quince	*2 oz flour*
4 oz mixed nuts (eg walnuts almonds brazils)	*2 oz light brown sugar*
1 small dsp cinnamon	*4 oz butter*
1 small dsp cardamom seeds	
1 tbsp sugar	
Oven heated to 180°C	*Medium baking dish*

Stew the quince and apple separately. To the stewing apple add cinnamon, ground cardamom seeds and sugar.
Combine both fruits in a baking dish.
Swirl the roughly chopped nuts in melted butter and sugar over a gentle heat until caramelised.
Sprinkle the nuts over the top of the fruit.
Combine the oats, flour and sugar and cut the butter through the dried ingredients to make a crumble mixture.
Spread over the fruit and nuts.
Bake for about 30 minutes until golden.

Endings of every kind form the warp and weft of our lives. Ever present though they are in one shape or another, many of us have far from simple feelings about them, and react in a variety of ways when faced with them.

There are those of us who embrace them and, with the scent of new horizons in our nostrils, might neither look back nor remember to say goodbye.

There are those of us who find the trepidations of the strange and new that lie inevitably on the other side of an ending a little daunting, and wish to linger with the familiar just as long as we are able.

There are those of us who focus on what we have lost and those of us who notice most what we are gaining.

The one who has precipitated an ending may feel quite differently about it from the one who feels they have been the unwilling recipient of the change.

There are both sides to this ending here.

Our cook, who views her life as a series of links in a chain, is trying to discover what shape the next link must be. There is the pleasure of anticipation in this, but also uncertainties. She is no longer anchored by the solidity of the Barn.

For those who find themselves without the Barn, there will be some who move on easily, and with pleasure, to try out different restaurants and cafés.

The very last thing the Barn would ever have intended to be was the answer to everyone's idea of an eating place.

But then there will be some who find that the final closing of the Barn has left an uncalled for space in their lives, a space that is not so easy to fill. It might leave a touch of regret that this unusual place is no more.

As the fly-on-the-wall I would like to include, for all those who are in the mood to celebrate the positive in any change and for all those who mourn a little, a grand finale of a pudding - a pudding, I consider, to end all puddings. Or as our cook describes it:

A pudding in a tutu.

A completely frivolous pudding; definitely one to make for high days and holidays or to cheer you up on a dismal day.

She and I both hope it brings you a smile.

Pudding in a Tutu

Meringue

4 egg whites

9 oz caster sugar

Oven heated to 180°C

1 dsp cornflour

1 tsp cream of tartar

Start beating the egg whites in a bowl and add the sugar blended with the cornflour and cream of tartar, a spoonful at a time, beating constantly until all the sugar has been added and you have a thick unctuous consistency.

Spread into two 10 inch rounds on a greased baking tray. Put in the middle of the heated oven. Leave for about 7 minutes and then look to check that the meringue is beginning to turn honey coloured.

Turn oven down to 100°C and leave for about another 1½ hours.

Lift and tap the meringue to make sure it is hard.

Filling

2 egg whites

4 oz icing sugar

8 oz soft butter

4 oz dark chocolate

Toasted flaked almonds

Put egg whites and sugar into a bowl over simmering water and whip until thick.

In another bowl melt the chocolate, either over hot water, or in the microwave.

Beat the egg whites with sugar into the butter gradually and then fold in the melted chocolate.

Leave to cool and to thicken enough to make a spreading consistency.

Layer between the two meringues and spread some on top.

Sprinkle with toasted flaked almonds.

An afterword from our cook

I hope you have enjoyed this collection of tales and recipes. I would like to say a truly heartfelt thank you to all my customers for not trying to 'squish' me into a box marked 'conform' and 'regimented'. I thank you, too, for trusting that the dish you exclaimed over weeks or months ago, which has reappeared on the blackboard, and which might have undergone some slippage in its reincarnation, will still be to your liking.

We agonised somewhat over the title - and took some straw polls. However, the 'tutu' seemed to capture the delight and exuberance with which I approach each dish so - Pudding in a Tutu it has become.

I should also like to acknowledge and thank the wide range of renowned chefs and cooks whose work I have admired over the years. Without in anyway wishing to replicate, I am mindful that some osmosis has probably occurred. I drew on numerous memories when I stood transfixed before stall upon stall of mouth-watering bounty, mostly in foreign lands, in order to conjure up what I hoped would be delicious fare for hungry folk at the Barn Café.

Tables and disclaimers

We hope you will forgive some of the eccentricities of measurement in this book as well as the decision to stick with imperial quantities. It is one of life's little ironies that a cook, who began her cooking life in France, should find herself measuring instinctively in the imperial system.

There are a number of conversion tables provided below which we hope will answer your every need.

1 dsp = 2 tsp (Why measure twice when once will do?)

Oven Temperatures

Oven temperatures in the book are set for a fan oven. If you have an electric oven without a fan you need to set the temperature a little higher than is suggested in the recipes, according to your manufacturer's instructions.

°C	Gas Mark
110	¼
120	½
140	1
150	2
160	3
180	4
190	5
200	6
220	7

Liquid Measurement

Fluid Ounces	Millilitres
2	55
5 (¼ pint)	150
10 (½ pint)	300
15 (¾ pint)	450
20 (1 pint)	600

Dry Weight

Ounces	Grams
1	25
2	50
3	75
4	100
5	150
6	175
7	200
8	225
9	250
10	275
11	300
12	350
13	375
14	400
15	425
16 (1 lb)	450

The conversions of dry and liquid quantities are to a recommended, rather than precise, metric equivalent.

Index by recipe name

Savoury

Sweet

Index by princpal ingredients

Spinach

Open Spinach Tart 52
Spinach Stuffed Sweet Peppers 20

Sweet Peppers

Garlic Chicken and Roasted Pepper Purée 30
Open Spinach Tart 52
Spinach Stuffed Sweet Peppers 20
Sweet Peppers with Goat's Cheese & Anchovy ..49

Sweet Potatoes

Aubergine Sambal 28
Vegetable Tagine 38

Tomato

Aubergine Provençal................................68
Broccoli with Attitude.............................25
Coq au Vin 34
Corsican Calamari 55
Fresh Tomato Soup 44
Garlic Chicken and Roasted Pepper Purée 30
Imam Bayildi 62
Vegetable Tagine 38

Walnut

Asparagus Tart.....................................37
Cucumber Soup 44
Coffee and Walnut Cake 10

Wine

Coq au Vin 34
Corsican Calamari 55
Pot Roast Beef 17